A Blond Boy with Buttercups

Kathleen Hollingworth

Illustrated by Andy Beck

Printed in England
by
G. H. Smith & Son
The Advertiser Office
Market Place, Easingwold
York YO61 3AB
Tel: 01347 821329
www.ghsmith.com

Published by the
Arkengarthdale Millennium Project
Contact Tel: 01748 884534

ISBN 0-9539215-2-2

Design and Typography
Graham White

Design Consultant
Richard Birks

To Ben
Adam & Thomas
My three fine sons

Ben

My eldest son, Ben, died of suicide on
3rd February 1998 aged twenty two
years. Since that time I have been
trying to find a way through the
indescribable pain and a meaning to life
again.

Ben's death is a hurt, a deep black hole,
that travels into me for eternity.

The pain of his death will be with me
forever.

Red Grouse

To the Memory of Rupert Brooke

He's gone
I do not understand
I only know that as he turned to go
and waved
In his young eyes a sudden glory shone
And I was dazzled by a sunset glow
And he was gone

W.W. Gibson

About this Book

This book has been written as an expression of my love for Ben. It is in part memoir, part diary, part memory, although the memories are mainly those given to me by Ben's friends and family. Many of my memories are sadly missing as if wiped by the horrific nature of his death. Fragments have come back and I am hopeful one day, encouraged by other parents who have suffered in a similar way, they will all come back. I have been told this can take many years.

When well meaning friends said to me that I would have my memories to comfort me I wanted to shout that I did not. My head was filled with too much pain. There was no room for happy memories.

I thank the dear people who gave me their memories and allowed me to use them in this book for I appreciate how personal they are. In doing so they could not have known how much they in turn would help me.

My book also includes poetry I have written since Ben's death and poetry that I have loved and which has had great meaning for me over the years. This poetry has now taken on a new meaning since Ben's death and some echo the universal effects of grief and loss.

This book is about the journey I was forced to embark upon because of my son's death. I could never have known how difficult and impossible the journey would be at times and I know I will be on this journey for the rest of my earthly life. However, I believe it is ultimately a journey of hope.

Ben's birth was a gift, one of the best gifts I have ever had. Adam and Tom are my others. He grew into a beautiful man, a caring and compassionate human being and was everything and more I could have hoped for. Ben gave me another gift, one only possible through his death. It is a gift, it goes without saying, I would give back instantly to have my beloved son alive but this can never happen. So, unwillingly, I have taken up this gift and treasure it. It is the absolute realisation of the impermanence of life and with that has come a great understanding and clarity. It is as if I have been allowed into the inner sanctum of all knowing. Death has lost its sting.

There are times when visiting Ben's grave I look at the spot where I will lie and am comfortable with this and look forward to embracing death when my time comes. In no way does it mean I do not value life. I value it perhaps more than most having experienced its fragility but I am totally at ease with death.

My husband and I would have been buried together but we have agreed he will now lie on Ben's right side and I will lie on his left.

Sealhouses, Arkengarthdale Photograph by Graham White

A Brief History

I have lived in Arkengarthdale with my husband Dave for twenty six years. Ben was two and a half years old when we moved into the dale in December 1977. Adam was born in June 1978 and Tom followed nearly three years later in March 1981. Perfection, three healthy sons and a beautiful place to live.

They were country children and walked miles exploring and discovering. They rode bikes, climbed hills, played in the woods and streams. They all went to the local village school where I have worked as the school secretary for eighteen years.

Ben was a deep thinker, a very spiritual person and a wonderful son. He was in a remote, beautiful place high on the moors and there was a spectacular sunset the evening he died. I had the film from his camera processed after his death and two of the prints were of sunsets taken from the moor where he worked as a gamekeeper.

At the inquest of Ben's death the verdict was open but I have come to the conclusion his death was suicide. In many ways this has complicated the grieving process and is a heavy burden to carry but it is a fact. I am not ashamed of this fact but am greatly saddened by it.

A Reflection by Lord Peel

I had the pleasure of knowing Ben when he came to work for me as a gamekeeper on the Grinton Estate. There was a certain composure about him which was unusual for one so young. His natural charm and dedication to his job shone through at all times, and all who met him seemed naturally drawn towards him. I felt that he was destined for good things, and, so like everyone else, felt a huge sense of loss when he left us.

He will always be remembered with great affection.

View from Lemon Gill towards Calver Hill and Arkengarthdale
(from a painting by Vic Smith. By kind permission of the Hazel Smith Gallery)

Mild the Mist Upon the Hill

Mild the mist upon the hill,
Telling not of storms to-morrow;
No; the day has wept its fill,
Spent its store of silent sorrow.

Oh, I'm gone back to the days of youth,
I am a child once more;
And 'neath my father's sheltering roof,
And near the old hall door,

I watch this cloudy evening fall,
After a day of rain:
Blue mists, sweet mists of summer pall
The horizon's mountain-chain.

The damp stands in the long, green grass
As thick as morning's tears;
And dreamy scents of fragrance pass
That breathe of other years.

Emily Brontë

*This was read at Ben's funeral
by Lord Peel*

In the Beginning

'Give sorrow words: the grief that does not speak
Whispers the o'er fraught heart, and bids it break.'

William Shakespeare

My eldest son, Ben, died of suicide on 3rd February 1998 aged twenty two years. Writing that sentence after nearly six years is very emotional and yet at the same time distant and unreal. Surely this event so huge, so horrendous couldn't possibly have happened to such an ordinary, loving family. It has a dreamlike quality about it and even after all this time part of me feels that one day I might wake from the nightmare.

In the weeks and months after my son's death I kept sane by walking, talking, crying and writing although not necessarily in that order. Some days I would walk miles across the moors where Ben spent most of his working life as a gamekeeper. I realise now I was searching for him and was certain I could find him if I searched long and hard enough. The Headkeeper on Lord Peel's estate took me to a spot where Ben had recently walked before his death and there in the mud was a footprint of his boot which convinced me I had only just missed him.

Some days the need to talk with friends and family was overriding as was their need to talk with me in order for us all to try and make sense of a senseless event. There were days when I could do nothing but weep uncontrollably and there were days when the urge to pick up a pen and scribble down the tumbling, chaotic thoughts that swam wildly in my head was overwhelming.

Writing was an instinctive need and I was to understand, much later down the path of grief, a very common expression of releasing pain. In fact all four of the activities I regularly participated in are normal and very much part of the grieving process.

While in the raw, deepest grief of the first two years, many times I felt I was on the verge of madness. If I didn't hold on tightly I felt I would go screaming over the edge into a bottomless black hole. Towards the end of this time I began sinking into a deep depression. Obviously the searching was futile and I became both mentally and physically weary of it. I began closing down and only doing what was expected of me and necessary but without any spark.

However, I still wanted to write. I needed to record and validate the pain.

It is interesting now as I read my 'Ben Poems', as I called them, how they mirrored the progression of the grieving process.

'Get me out of winter
I'm drowning in the darkness
of a bleak and half-dead landscape'

This was written as I approached the first winter without Ben. The blackness was swallowing me up and I didn't know how I could survive without light. However, by the time Spring of the following year had arrived I couldn't bear the light that had seemed so intolerably hard to leave behind in the Autumn.

'The light of Spring is too bright for my eyes
Leave me in the darkness where my grey heart lives.'

Ben was a good looking, sensitive young man. He had friends, a family who adored him, a job he loved, a car, a future and even a pension. One of the most difficult things to do was to accept a cheque from his pension company as the next of kin of the deceased. How every part of me shouted "This is Ben's money for his retirement, to make his old age comfortable. Please, please someone take it for I cannot bear to." But of course I did and felt Ben had died again for me as his future security now was gone.

I was told that shortly before Ben died he gave a donation to the RSPCA after reading of a cruelty case, involving a dog, in his newspaper. This act so identified my son with the compassionate person he was. I now regularly give donations to various animal charities as a means of assuaging the guilt I feel at having to accept his pension money.

As I look back on six years of disbelief, shock, pain, tears, madness, guilt and the many other emotions that grief entails, I realise how far I have travelled on the hardest journey of my life. I also realise I will be on this journey for the rest of my earthly life. Such is the price of knowing one of the purest and most exquisite of all loves, that of a mother for her child.

Ben heather burning.   Photograph by Lord Peel

Where are you?

Where are you my love,
my son, my life
in the winter silence of your tomb
clothed and warm with boots and heather
familiar landmarks all around
near a constant stream that flows forever?

Where are you my love
my son, my life
high upon your purple moor
do you see the peewits fly
mad with joy at spring's beginning
can you hear the curlew's cry?

Where are you my love,
my son, my life
striding knee-high through the heather
stick and dog to heel
scented summer skies above you
tell me, can you feel?

Where are you my love,
my son, my life
underneath a harvest moon
bathed in ethereal silver light
do you hear the soft wind sighing
across your moor this autumn night?

Where are you my love,
my son, my life?
You are everywhere
safe in hearts of friends and brothers
fishing in the silent pools
walking the high moors
where you are one day I'll be too
then forever love I'll be with you.

Kathleen Hollingworth

Calver Hill from Arkengarthdale and Curlews

Carrying the Load

The only way I believe we truly grow is through adversity. Ben's death was adversity of the worst kind and for my other two sons to be confronted with the suicide of their brother was almost more than they could bear. As a mother one of my greatest pains was being unable to take away their pain. Although it was a natural instinct there was no way I could do this for it was their pain, their journey.

For an hour before any other family member knew, even my husband, I alone tried to absorb the fact that my eldest son was dead. I remember sitting totally alone apart from our dogs while the police, assured by me that I wanted to be on my own, went off in search of my husband. In the dusk of a February late afternoon I wanted to halt time so that no one else need know and feel the absolute wretchedness of this sickening reality.

For me to learn later that Ben had been dead nearly a whole twenty four hours before anyone knew was devastating. No one should be alone at the moment of death and yet not only had my son died alone but had been alone in death for so long before he was found.

My husband eventually arrived home tailed by police and the news was broken to him. He fell against the wall and the police and I helped him into the house. We then told Adam when he came home from work. He wouldn't let me touch or hold him and went to his room and sat in the dark for hours. My youngest son was at college about fifty miles away. A good friend drove my husband and I there as we were too traumatised to drive. The overriding memory of the journey home was the silence and my youngest son clenching and unclenching his jaw. He sat separate and tense lost in his own pain and thoughts.

As I look at them now, six years later, how proud I am that they are still good, rounded individuals and both have a great sense of humour. Above all I am proud they are caring, compassionate people with no bitterness.

I have no doubt there are times that are hard for my sons to bear, as is the case for both my husband and I. However, it is their journey and as much as I would like to step in and carry their load I have realised I am unable to do this for their difficult journey will make them who they are - strong, capable, compassionate men.

Red Grouse in flight

To My Son

Son, I am powerless to protect you though
My heart for yours beats ever anxiously,
Blind through piteous darkness you must go,
And find with a new vision lights I see.
If it might ease you I would bear again
All the old suffering that I too have known,
All sickness, terror, and the spirit's pain,
But you, alas, must make those three your own.
Yes, though I beat away a thousand fears
And forge your armour without flaw or chink,
And though I batter Heaven with my prayers,
Yet from a self-filled cup of grief you drink.
Oh, son of woman, since I gave you breath
You walk alone through life to face your death.

Dorothea Eastwood

This was read at Ben's funeral by my cousin Ian Johnson

The First few Days

People cautiously approached me in those first few days after Ben's death expecting a mad and demented wreck but shock kept me absolutely distanced from reality. This is obviously nature's way of allowing the mind to cope with unimaginable horror.

You could see the puzzled look on people's faces as I behaved almost normally.

"Would you like a cup of tea? Come and see the wonderful flowers. Look at this beautiful card."

They didn't see me weeks later, broken with pain, after discovering a receipt in Ben's jacket for the last Christmas presents he bought us.

Ben with his cousin Sarah

A Blond Boy with Buttercups

Get me out of winter
I'm drowning in the darkness
of a bleak and half-dead landscape
as autumn fades and
winter's grasp takes hold
immobilising all life in its path

My heart is half-dead too
It still beats
but is choked with pain and longing
for a blond boy with buttercups
I knew long ago

He was my son

Kathleen Hollingworth

Chapel of Rest

Ben was brought to the Chapel of Rest in Reeth on Sunday 8th February and lay there until his burial on the 11th February. I remember being mildly puzzled each day when we went to see him that he had never moved. He was lying, sleeping in the same position. So obvious, but not to a mother in such deep shock that the full horror of the reality hadn't even begun to penetrate my mind.

Each day I expected him to have turned over, shuffled around in his sleep but he was always lying in the same position.

One of the saddest memories I have of that precious time, the last days of being able to touch and kiss my dead son, was his grandmothers and aunts coming to see him. They instinctively took hold of his ice hands and began to rub them as you would a child's hands coming in from the cold on a snowy day. We will rub and warm them up, we will make it better, and I silently thanked them.

And while the trials of life keep on occurring, Ben lies in his grave and I am tormented. Will this always be so? Would it have been easier to have had him cremated? I wonder now why, at the time of his death, we didn't consider the alternative to burial. I'm sure we would have come to the same conclusion but why no discussion, no weighing up the pros and cons, as if there can be any pros. The pros of having your child buried, how crazy that sounds. And always Ben lies sleeping on for eternity.

Adam and Tom's Involvement

I didn't insist but gently cajoled Adam and Tom into going to see Ben when he was brought to the Chapel of Rest in Reeth. I instinctively knew that it would be regretted later in life if they didn't go. Of the four days Ben was there Adam went every day. I think there was much to say whereas Tom went once.

Adam and Tom were young men when Ben died but because death is so alien to youth they were in no way remotely prepared and could not comprehend death although confronted with it in its starkest and most brutal reality - their brother lying in a coffin in Reeth after shooting himself.

I believe children of whatever age should have an involvement with the whole death process on a level suitable for them. Adam and Tom had a great deal of involvement in the events following Ben's death and this has been a help, a healing and a comfort to them.

Tom insisted on some of John Lennon's music being played at Ben's funeral as he knew Ben had recently bought a CD of his music and loved it. Tom also went with his good friend John Sunter and built a stone man at Lemon Gill, shortly after Ben's death.

Adam went alone and planted many daffodil bulbs in a circle around the spot on the moor where Ben died. These now grow in a wonderful profusion every Spring and are an oasis of colour and hope in the wildness of the moor.

28

The Stone Man at Lemon Gill. Built by Tom and John
(reproduced by kind permission of the Darlington & Stockton Times)

Fire in My Heart
Ice in My Veins

Word of your death greeted me like
a wave of despair
drowning out
a bonfire of hope.

The fire in my heart gave way
to the ice running through my veins.

Your death caught me from behind,
like cold fingers gripping the back of my neck
forcing my heart to crack
open.
Your death is the fire that ravages
through the forests
of my soul,
leaving black and grey ashes in its wake.
In the shade suddenly drawn down around,
I will plant memories of you
and inhale their sweet smell in the spring.
The fire in my heart thawed
the ice running through my veins.

Life will always follow after death
as even the longest, darkest of nights
are followed by the light of day.

David G. Traisman

Digging the Grave

*'For life and death are one, even as the river
and the sea are one'*

From - The Prophet by Kahlil Gibran

At the time of Ben's death my husband, as well as running his own dry stone walling business, was also the local gravedigger. Of course no one expected him to dig Ben's grave but he made the decision to do this as it was the last thing he could do for Ben.

I remember walking down to see him the day before the funeral with my good friend Marguerita Barningham and him smiling at us as he stood shoulder height in the grave. It shocked me how far down it went. It was a moment of total unreality. A week ago we had been a complete family and yet now my husband was smiling at me from our son's grave.

I cannot begin to imagine how it must have felt knowing in a day his eldest son would lie forever in this earth he had so recently dug.

The evening of Ben's burial I asked my husband to dig Ben up again so I could have one last night with him. I was absolutely distraught and in some state of madness. Of course he refused.

As the days passed I was extremely distressed at the thought of Ben lying in his grave, especially if it rained or was very cold. People said to me, "It's his body, his shell, Ben isn't there," and although on one level I understood this, my heart told me something else. Then a very discerning friend said that I had every right to feel so distraught. Ben's spirit had gone from his body but it was still his body, the body I had borne, held, kissed, loved better than life itself and therefore it was incredibly precious.

I felt an aversion to his grave because it was just too painful to know my son's body was a few feet under the earth on which I stood and I couldn't reach him. So I focused on the place he died, Lemon Gill. I now feel a need to be near Ben's grave too. It is a softer feeling, a feeling of defeated resignation. I like to think his body is safe in Arkengarthdale churchyard and his spirit is free on the moors he loved.

St.Mary's Church, Arkengarthdale   Photograph by Graham White

The Noble Nature

It is not growing like a tree
In bulk, doth make Man better be;
Or standing long an oak, three hundred year,
To fall a log at last, dry, bald, and sere:
A lily of a day
Is fairer far in May,
Although it fall and die that night -
It was the plant and flower of Light.
In small proportions we just beauties see:
And in short measures life may perfect be.

Ben Jonson

*This poem was given to me by my good friend Marguerita Barningham shortly
after Ben's death as we walked down to Arkengarthdale churchyard to see my
husband who was digging Ben's grave.*

Oak leaves and acorns

Frozen Tarn
..a memory

Iremember a small, mitted child's hand in mine. Ben and I went exploring the moor opposite Shaw Farm on a freezing winter's day. High on the moor we came to a tarn and stopped silent at the sight. There stood a dead sheep encased in the frozen waters with glazed, frosted eyes, looking ahead as if it was about to step out from its icy prison.

It is a vision that comes back to haunt me now as I remember my dead son's perfect eye. I gently lifted his eyelid as he lay in the Chapel of Rest with a courage, borne of a curiosity, that would defeat me now.

Shaw Farm

Here I am
..a memory by Rosalind Earl

Ben first came to see us with his Mum and Dad and baby brother
Adam. When Ben joined us at Arkengarthdale School in Spring
1980 he was still four years old and at least two years younger than
any of the other children who ranged in age from six to eleven.
There were no other children due to begin in the reception year with
him. He was also my first new entrant and a new venture for me.

At first the experience seemed to be quite daunting for both Ben
and myself, but I needn't have worried as he made himself at home
very quickly.

The other children in the school were delighted to have a little
one to attend to, and the main worry became that of making sure he
wasn't spoilt by the over indulgence of the other children. There had
to be enough time and equipment available for him to engage in
suitable play activities both on his own and alongside the other
younger children.

On a daily basis I would be involved with teaching groups, having
set Ben up with an activity. The other children would be working
away and then a little head would pop up under my arm saying "Here
I am" and then he would settle with me to watch what the others
were doing. This little phrase of his as he made contact with me
became a byword in my family as a way of announcing our arrivals
into many situations.

At the end of the day most of the children went home by bus or
were collected by car. Ben and his family lived up on the moorside,
not on anyone else's route. Sometimes there was a delay in collecting

him and we would stand at the gate and watch the van's progress down the steep, twisty road. Ben had a very matter of fact approach to this, not at all anxious about being the last. In fact those few moments alone with him were very valuable, as we would chat about the day and what he had done and enjoyed.

I have warm memories of Ben and in those early days of my first headship at Arkengarthdale School he lightened and enhanced my daily life with his charm and enthusiasm.

Rosalind Earl was Headteacher at Arkengarthdale School from Sept.1979 until Dec.1981

Arkengarthdale School

Walking Away

It is eighteen years ago, almost to the day -
A sunny day with the leaves just turning,
The touch-lines new-ruled - since I watched you play
Your first game of football, then, like a satellite
Wrenched from its orbit, go drifting away

Behind a scatter of boys, I can see
You walking away from me towards the school
With the pathos of a half-fledged thing set free
Into the wilderness, the gait of one
Who finds no path where the path should be.

That hesitant figure, eddying away
Like a winged seed loosened from its parent stem,
Has something I never quite grasp to convey
About nature's give-and-take - the small, the
    scorching
Ordeals which fire one's irresolute clay.

I have had worse partings, but none that so gnaws at
    my mind still. Perhaps it is roughly
Saying what God alone could perfectly show -
How selfhood begins with a walking away,
And love is proved in the letting go.

C Day Lewis

This poem was read at Ben's funeral by my cousin Ian Johnson

Saturday 7th March 1998

I woke at 7.00 a.m. to the churning stomach and sick fluttering feeling that thumps in and I am instantly alert with Ben consuming all my thoughts. The pain is dissipating into an emptiness so vast, so hollow it is without end and I feel an overwhelming sadness. Sadness seems to be the word to describe my feelings now. It completely surrounds me and obliterates all else from view. A sadness that weighs me down so that I can hardly walk and move. Sadness for what has happened and for what should have been Ben's future.

This sadness felt no better than the tortuous pain. I haven't ever been tortured but I liken losing a beloved child to torture as there is nothing one can do except suffer the pain until the body's natural anaesthetic cuts in to allow some respite. Like a prisoner knowing it will begin again but not when, the uncertainty and fear of the pain returning was almost as bad. And after such bouts of torture my body was left weary and near exhaustion.

The 'good' days were now the grey days when I could function to some degree. In the past the grey days were the worst and happened only occasionally. Now they were to be welcomed.

It was tantalising to allow myself one second of transportation to a time without sorrow or sadness. I would see a gamekeeper's Landrover coming up the road and in a momentary indulgence imagine it was Ben coming for an evening meal with us again.

In the early days I was cushioned by shock and unreality. It was only when the shock began to wear off that I was confronted with the absolute awfulness and reality and then it became hard to live.

As the weeks passed there seemed to be a pattern emerging when the pain would become so intense I couldn't distinguish between the physical and mental hurt, they were inseparable. I felt an intense physical pain somewhere deep inside near my heart and yet the pain was also in my head. How could I still be alive and walking and going about life's business, albeit in a detached way, when I was suffering such intense pain and misery? Then there would be periods of flatness, almost a calm, with the sadness covering every crevice of life until I felt I would suffocate under the weight of it all. However, these times of calm were the respite, the good days, where I could gather my breath ready for the next onslaught. I likened this process to giving birth. There were similarities between suffering the pain of Ben's death and the pain of bringing him into the world. The intense labour pains and then the breathers where I could gather myself until the next wave of pain. All the time pushing until this new life would become one of the most important people in my life. This is where the similarity ended as there would be no ending to this death - a pain to be endured for all time until my death.

About nine months after Ben's death when I was well into this pattern of grief it began to change. I was aware of something happening but it was so subtle, so gradual that it was hard to describe. Tim Tunley, our vicar, asked me one day at school how I felt and I couldn't describe it. It was a feeling, a pain without words.

Whereas before I knew where the arrows of pain were coming from suddenly they seemed to be attacking from different directions at different times, crashing down and not allowing any respite, not a moment of peace. Previously I was in an ordered phase of grief but this was chaotic, out of control and I couldn't understand what was happening. But of course I now know this is grief.

And throughout all this I constantly worried about Ben. Where was he? If he wasn't here he must be somewhere, but where, WHERE? Frantically I searched, read books of every description on death. Was he in heaven with God, part of the universe, here with us, up at Lemon Gill, wandering, lost, suffering, suffering at our suffering?

Oh to have an unquestionable faith.

Time does not bring Relief

Time does not bring relief; you all have lied
Who told me time would ease me of my pain!
I miss him in the weeping of the rain;
I want him at the shrinking of the tide;
The old snows melt from every mountain-side,
And last year's leaves are smoke in every lane;
But last year's bitter loving must remain
Heaped on my heart, and my old thoughts abide.
There are a hundred places where I fear
To go, - so with his memory they brim.
And entering with relief some quiet place
Where never fell his foot or shone his face
I say, "There is no memory of him here!"
And so stand stricken, so remembering him.

Edna St. Vincent Millay

Forty Days and Forty Nights

Those early days, weeks and months were our forty days and nights in the wilderness. We were suffering the same ultimate degree of pain but it was different for each one of us. We were separate as if in protective bubbles. We could see each other but couldn't communicate beyond this.

After our time in this emotional wilderness, tentatively and gradually, our relationships began to resume. Some of the communication, however, was upsetting and shocking to a family normally sane and loving. But of course I wanted what was impossible. I wanted my husband to bring Ben back to me. I screamed at him, shrieked until my throat hurt and I fell breathless on the floor. "Bring Ben back. Bring him back to me." But he was helpless, either to bring him back or console me in my all consuming pain - a mother desperately searching for her first born child.

I would say "Ben is dead, Ben is dead", over and over again as I was cooking, washing up, walking the dogs. Sometimes I would say it in my head, sometimes I would whisper "Ben is dead". Sometimes I would say it out loud and startle myself with the sound and strangeness of the words. No matter how often or how loud I repeated the words it still didn't make it real. I was like a young child trying to read and understand a Latin phrase. It was totally beyond comprehension. The words made no sense and yet deep within me I was beginning to understand the horror of their meaning.

Watching the pain of the people around me whom I loved was an extra layer adding to the despair. How easy, when a child is small, it is to wipe a tear, wash a graze, cuddle it all better.

How absolutely impossible to chip into the dark, unbearable pain of a son who has taken the guilt of the world upon his shoulders, simply because there was more sibling rivalry between one brother than another.

Tom and Adam - taken on Tom's 21st Birthday

To My Mountain

Since I must love your north
of darkness, cold, and pain,
the snow, the lovely glen,
let me love true worth,

the strength of the hard rock,
the deafening stream of wind
that carries sense away
swifter than flowing blood.

Heather is harsh to tears
and the rough moors
give the buried face no peace
but make me rise,

and oh, the sweet scent, and purple skies!

Kathleen Raine

*This poem, which became prophetic, was pinned
to our family notice board for years.
Lord Peel's son, Ashton Clanfield,
read it at Ben's funeral.*

Peat hag

The Following Year

In the year following Ben's death my husband immersed himself in the garden while I looked on aghast at his energy, and to be frank, with total incomprehension at caring about it. However, three years later, the garden became my solace and I too found a great comfort in watching and helping nature's cycle.

In the days and weeks after his death I had a great need to watch the only video we have of Ben's twenty first birthday. Just the sound of it had my husband running, not only from the room but sometimes the house, so impossible and unbearable it was for him. He has never been able to watch it for also on it is his father who died a year after Ben. He suffered a stroke two weeks after Ben's death and never recovered.

There are no right or wrong ways in the grieving process. We must do whatever we can to survive whilst trying to be aware of the pain and distress of others and allowing them their space and time to do whatever helps them survive.

Spring 1999

The light of spring is too bright for my eyes
Leave me in the darkness where my grey heart lives
It sears my heart to see new life begin
And I cannot bear to hear the sounds of spring

Why do joyous birds sing overhead
Don't they know my son is dead?

Kathleen Hollingworth

Peewits

A Year of Seasons

I wasn't aware of Spring coming or going or even Summer and then Autumn. It was only when I was back in the dark nights and gloom of Winter that I realised nearly a year of seasons had passed and somehow I must have been part of them.

I grew into Winter and the season suited my mind - dead, bleak but not without a small hope that the sun would shine again. How indomitable is the human spirit. But I had to keep going for Adam and Tom. They were to be my salvation.

Hawthorn Tree near Lemon Gill

The Den
..a memory by Colin Atkinson

I got to know Ben when he moved into the dale with his family when he was two or three. We bonded and became close friends and spent a lot of our time together. As we got older we went riding our BMX bikes through the dales at weekends. You could say we were the terrible twosome.

I remember the day we built a den out of stone in Faggergill wood. It is still standing to this day, eighteen years on.

Even though we were a similar age, Ben was only a few months older, he was always like a big brother and looked out for me. He was gentle and caring if he wasn't taking the mick with his great sense of humour.

When we were old enough we went out drinking together and socialising. On many occasions we would go out for a drive. We shared the same interest in nice cars. There was one day we went for a drive near Alston. The snow was deep and Ben jumped into it and went up to his waist. I can remember laughing so much. I'll never forget his sense of humour.

Colin was a lifelong friend of Ben. After Ben died Colin worked in gamekeeping for a while then went working and travelling in Australia for a year. He returned to Arkengarthdale where he now works.

Lemon Gill

The year after Ben died I continually searched for him. I walked miles over the moors where he once walked, sometimes exploring the old childhood haunts, but spending more time in the areas he had recently worked and of course often going to the place he died, Lemon Gill. A track leads from the road for about a mile climbing steadily and then the stone men come into view. Tom and a friend built one near to where Ben died shortly after his death and since then others have appeared as if standing guard.

One night shortly after Ben's burial, in an absolute panic to find him, I begged my husband to take me to Lemon Gill. We drove there in his vehicle eventually leaving the track and going across the moor. He shone the headlights until I reached the spot where Ben had died and then switched them off. I stood in the darkness and felt the night against my face and Ben slipping away. If only I'd come sooner.

The only other time my husband and I have been to Lemon Gill at night was on the Millennium Eve. We both felt a great need to be there. We even took Ben's spaniel, Brock, who thought it was wonderful to be experiencing another walk so late at night.

The evening will stay with me always. As midnight struck on the pick up's radio the sky lit up around us for miles into the distance. Here we were completely alone, high on a remote Swaledale moor in total darkness and yet experiencing this firework extravaganza which surrounded us. It was magical and surreal and I felt Ben close to me.

New Year

I feel the panic rising
as the old year nears its close
For as we move towards midnight
I know you can never be part of the new year
For a short while you belonged
in the year near departing
and I want it never to end
though it bursts with so much sorrow
I can't leave you behind
You will come with me
Safe in my heart
you will come with me into the new year

Kathleen Hollingworth

Boyhood Freedom
..a memory by Andrew Barningham

'Where the pools are bright and deep,
Where the grey trout lies asleep,
Up the river and o'er the lea,
That's the way for Billy and me.'

From 'A Boy's Song' by James Hogg

When we were very young, I can't remember exactly how old we were, Ben, my brother Stuart and I went for a bike ride to Tan Hill. Ben, being a year older, was the expedition leader. This was a big adventure for me as I had never been to Tan Hill before.

When we got there I remember feeling a bit nervous but thought, 'stick with Ben, he will keep us right.' We all got half a Coca-Cola and shared a basket of chips. Ben put a song on the jukebox 'Ride on time' by Blackbox.

Whenever I hear that song it always reminds me of being at Tan Hill with Ben, of our boyhood freedom and happy times.

Andrew now travels the world with his work as an engineer
and remains a good friend to Adam and Tom.

Tan Hill Inn

June 5th 1999
Arkengarthdale Sports Day
The day after Ben's 24th Birthday

I walked down to Ben's grave this afternoon at 2 o'clock and met Jenny who was upset that Darius had missed the fancy dress parade. We walked a short distance together, chatting, and then parted company. As I got nearer to the churchyard I heard the guns going off at the clay pigeon shoot in the nearby sports field. The sound ricocheted around the hills. I wondered what sort of noise the gun going off in Ben's mouth would have made. I could also hear the shouts and sounds of the children in the distance together with strains of the local brass band.

'Into my heart an air that kills
From yon far country blows:
What are those blue remember'd hills,
What spires, what farms are those?

That is the land of lost content,
I see it shining plain,
The happy highways where I went
And cannot come again'

A.E. Housman

The sounds were the sounds of my boys years ago, running the races, winning the prizes and the realisation that I couldn't ever be part of that again was almost more than I could bear. I might someday go to the show again but not yet.

I met Avril outside the church with a bunch of white lilac she had picked for Stephen's grave. It was good to have her there as a companion even though we were both there for the saddest of reasons. Our first born sons had died and were lying in this churchyard. How it made me feel less alone.

The churchyard and surrounding meadows were ablaze with buttercups and clover and other wild flowers. I was dazzled when the sun shone out on it all from behind the clouds. Ben's grave looked beautiful with the birthday flowers all over it, especially the roses. A black and white spider moved across his grave and some sort of gnat with gossamer wings was on his headstone. How could my beautiful son be lying in his grave when the world around was so alive?

Desolation

There's a desolation in my soul
where the winds of time
whisper of a joy complete
echoes of children's voices
are calling down the years
So long ago
So

long

ago

Kathleen Hollingworth

Ben, Thomas and Adam. 1982

54

Ben, left - with Sarah, Adam and myself

Childhood
..memories by Sarah Leigh Johnson

Sometimes when I think of Ben it happens completely unexpectedly and takes me by surprise. Last week a beautiful Spring day with a clear blue sky took me back to Ben's twenty first birthday, to a different life almost. It seems much harder to sit and try to remember Ben. Where could I start? For the whole of my life Ben has been part of this world. The memories are hard to separate into individual events, it is as though there is too much to remember.

When I was a young child Ben was the brother I would love to have had. One particular day stands out, perhaps because I can still remember the way I felt that day. Ben and I were heading off with some of his friends to play in the stream. It was a hot day and it was blissful to feel the cool water on my feet and pick up the smooth stones. I was slightly overawed by Ben who seemed so at ease in this natural world which felt almost foreign to me. On the way home we had a steep bank to climb and Ben and his friends bounded up without hesitation, totally fearless, whilst I picked my way up slowly and less sure of myself. I was torn between admiration and the irrational panic that I would be left behind. Even now I can recall the relief when I saw Ben stop and look behind to see where I was. Relief became thankfulness when I saw that he was making his way back down to help me.

Part of the reason that I think this stands out in my mind is because the quiet, kind way that he helped me is the way I always think of Ben. On a different level I think this memory is so strong because for me Ben is forever connected to the dale, the two are inseparable and each as much a part of the other.

Many of my childhood memories of Ben seem to be a blend of all the Sunday afternoons that we spent at our grandparents home in Moray Close, Peterlee and the holidays in Arkengarthdale. These times genuinely felt like events, something that I would write about on Monday in school. Ben being there meant games and fun and I am so lucky that I can remember lots of days like these. Days spent in make believe worlds like the time a film crew arrived in the dale and we followed them around with 'cameras' made of Lego, totally convinced we were helping them. Looking back now this itself seems like make believe, it could be another life that I am writing about.

I have re-written this so many times because I wanted to be sure that I had it clear in my own mind, and every time I have written about Ben the same emotions run through me. There is, of course, deep and real sadness because a wonderful blue sky reminds me how much Ben is missing and how much he is missed. But there is also a gladness, a pride that I knew such a beautiful person and that he has left me with memories that can make me smile.

Sarah Leigh Johnson is Ben's cousin. She now lives and works in London with her fiancé, Jed. They visit Arkengarthdale as often as they can.

Letting Go

For many months after Ben's death I was terrified to let Adam and Tom out of my sight but they were young men and I couldn't contain them. I had to let them go and live their lives. However I couldn't stop the irrational panic if they were late home or had changed their plans and had been unable to let me know immediately.

Tom went mountain biking on his own many times after Ben's death and once after a puncture and delay in returning I was convinced he had been murdered. Every thought was the very worst and I felt unable to have any trust in life.

This sounds like madness now but grief is a kind of madness.

Grief

Grief
I know you well
my constant companion
familiar and comforting
almost a friend
at first the shock
leaving me swimming
in a sea of desolation
so alone
so separate
even from the ones I loved the best
then
as the layers of shock were peeled away was
pain
raw agonising pain
so unbearable
so indescribable
some days I'd howl
like a wild wounded animal
not knowing where such unrecognisable sounds came from
some days I'd rock in silence and pray for oblivion
then came nothingness
no feeling, no pain,
no sadness, no future,
and this was as bad as pain
or perhaps worse

at least pain was a feeling, a reaction
and I knew I was still alive
but of course this was sinking
into the trough of depression
a woman beaten into submission
oh yes Grief
I know you well

Kathleen Hollingworth

Stone Man

A June Evening in the Year 2000
..a memory

On a June evening in the year 2000 my husband and I went to Ben's grave with flowers. As we arrived a pheasant was silently moving around the headstones, quite at one with the surroundings, totally oblivious to us. We stood for a moment quietly watching.

I thought it would please Ben. He would be happy with this.

Cock Pheasant

Churchyard

It used to be an occasional Sunday afternoon pastime
wandering through the stones
pondering the fate of those
lying beneath the silent turf
How well I know the fate
of this beloved boy who lies below
but not the reason why
I walk the well-worn track
with my posies of heartache
and wish with all my being
I had no need of this churchyard

Kathleen Hollingworth

Daffodils

Tears

For about two years following Ben's death there were tears at some point of every day. I became tired of tears. There were tears always for Ben but the tears mingled with tears for earthquake victims, for road and rail crash casualties. There were tears for starving children, for abused children and animals. There were also tears for the crushed bodies of rabbits on the country roads.

I became so weary of tears and sadness and grief and yet there was never any way of circumnavigating it, or dismissing it and leaving it behind. It was something I had to learn to live with. While at times in the early days I was so tired of the tears, as time progressed sometimes I longed for them as my safety valve.

Towards the end of June 2000 I hadn't cried for weeks. I wanted to but the tablets blunted my feelings. I felt desperately sad but the tears wouldn't come and with them release. Simon, a friend of Ben, telephoned one summer evening in late June to speak to Adam and Tom. The last time I had spoken to him on the phone was a few weeks after Ben died as he was leaving for Australia. I had sobbed and sobbed. Hearing his voice again after two years took me back to that last phone call and the hysterical tears.

For the rest of the evening my tears flowed. I had no control over them.

Ben's Smile
..a memory by Claire Davies

I didn't know Ben for very long. I met him when I was seventeen and he was twenty one. He was tall, good looking and easy going and I was instantly attracted to him. Ben was always happy, always smiling and he never had a bad word to say about anyone. My most vivid memory of him was his smile.

He was very ambitious. We spent a lot of time talking about the future and he had many ideas of what he wanted to do. I remember one particular night he said he was going to leave the country to work as a park ranger in the States. I laughed at him as he had a different idea every week but I liked this quality about him. He was different from everyone else around the dale.

He was only twenty one but Ben knew everything, or so he thought. He would lecture me on what clubs and pubs to go to, what to wear, where to shop. He thought he was a style icon and I went along with this. Ben was sensitive, fun-loving and seemed so sure of himself and that's why I liked him so much.

But the thing about Ben I will always remember is his smile.

Claire became a friend of Ben when he moved into his flat opposite Claire's home. Claire now teaches in Bedford and is a good friend of Adam and Tom.

Three Fine Sons

My father died
and life stopped for a while
Three fine sons and a husband
called me back to life
With open heart and open arms
I held on to life
and found happiness again
Then my son died
My beautiful, blue eyed, first born son
On a moortop bathed in a rosy splendour
he said goodbye to life
Two fine sons and a husband
are calling me back to life
With open heart and open arms
I am desperately trying to hold on
But how can I ever know happiness again?

Kathleen Hollingworth

I Feel Frightened

I feel frightened when I look back to the past for in looking back I glimpse the happiness of an intact family. I feel physically sick when my thoughts go back to the week Ben died. At the time I cleaned the house, washed clothes, prepared his funeral, all with such energy. But of course I was in shock, that marvellous state that allowed me to function and stay alive and sane. Now looking back to that time from the present I cannot believe I achieved so much in those early days and weeks but I look back now without the anaesthetic of shock.

I also feel frightened when I look to the future for in looking forward I see an old woman of eighty who has lived on this earth thirty four years without her beloved son and that doesn't seem possible. And so I stand semi frozen in the present, like a rabbit caught in headlights, wondering where to run. There is nowhere, but by cherishing the past and finding good things in the future then perhaps the present will be tolerable.

Since Ben's death I have no expectations of ever knowing happiness again and so when small unexpected 'gifts' happen I am surprised and uplifted.

Hare

Tom's Birthday

We had red balloons
and a cake with twenty one candles
Happy Birthday Dear Tom
We told you how proud we were
to have you as our son
and how we love you
But this had all been said before
to another son in another world
Were those carefully chosen words believed
or was fate waiting in the wings even then
ready to pounce with stealthy black fingers
that would pierce and crush our hearts
The video camera records
the same joyous scene
over and over again
Happy Birthday families
Why then do I feel as guilty
as if I had pulled the trigger?

Kathleen Hollingworth

The Last Day
.. a memory by John Baker

Friday the 30th January 1998 was the last day I spent with Ben.

I had recently withdrawn from university and wasn't working so a days beating at my Dad's pheasant shoot was easy money and meant I had to get out of bed. It was a chilly day and as usual I wasn't dressed for the occasion. Once I was mistaken for an anti-blood saboteur and removed from the moor. Ben would always take the mickey out of the way I dressed. I remember Ben purchasing a Gortex jacket and trousers. He had expensive tastes and these cost an absolute fortune! I remember asking him if they were any good. He said he'd tested them in the bath by wearing them and throwing water over himself, confirming they were very water resistant. I can picture him doing this with a big grin across his face. This was something Ben did a lot - smile.

Going back to the day's beating. It had been a top day with Ben and during the day Ben mentioned that there was a disco being held at the Buck Hotel that night, which in those days was a real highlight and something to look forward to. We planned the girls that we'd pull, the usual subject, although this is as far as it would get for me - talking about it, unlike Ben who was a real dark-horse when it came to the ladies.

We met up later that evening and from what I remember other friends, Colin Atkinson, Nick Guy and Guy Hird were also there propping up the bar in the Buck. Ben's mood had changed dramatically from the one he was in earlier. He was very quiet and reserved and wasn't responding to the usual banter we were all having.

I also noticed Ben wasn't drinking alcohol but he would either get so drunk that he could hardly stand, one night losing a shoe on the stagger home from a boozy night, or he would drink Britvic and lemonade. I don't think he ever found the shoe. I guess the thing I found so strange about his mood was that he had been so up for the night out and yet now was so reserved. Maybe he knew it was to be the last night out with his mates.

Ben suddenly decided he was going home but bearing in mind it was only about 10 o'clock I stood in his way to stop him. I told him I'd buy him a drink but he declined abruptly and said he'd hit me if I didn't let him pass. I reminded him that I was staying at his flat and he said he would leave the door open.

At the end of the night, very drunk, I went back to Ben's flat to find the door locked. The obvious thing to do was to wake him up. He answered the door, let me in and went straight back to bed while I made myself a nest on the floor in the living room.

The following morning I was woken by a cheesy smell, it was a sock on my face and I knew it was one of mine. The sock slowly worked it's way into my mouth and I realised it was Ben. I removed the sock and he stood there looking at me with that big beaming smile on his face.

Ben was going up to a nearby farm early that morning to cut juniper trees. His mood was good again and such a contrast to the night before. I got up and left.

All day Saturday I thought about the night before and what had happened with Ben. It was so bizarre. Ben had never threatened to hit me before. I was worried about him and decided to call round before I went out. Ben was doing something he took very seriously and loved, crossword competitions. He was always doing these in his spare time as he thought he could make cash from it.

I asked him if he was OK and he said he was fine. He didn't want to come out for a drink as he had the crosswords to do and there was a film he wanted to watch. Ben seemed happy so I left him to it.

This was the last time I saw Ben alive and what happened four days later can never be explained or understood.

John went on to get his degree and after working in London as an estate agent, recently moved back to Arkengarthdale. He remains a good friend to Adam and Tom.

Woodcock

LtoR Peter Richardson, John Baker, Ben and Kevin Hutchinson
Photograph by Tony Williams taken five days before Ben died.

Circles

I have
come to know
that life is a journey
going full circle for the old
woman of ninety to the day old
child, the diminishing light enfolds
the remnants of the day and soon
after we take our last breath
the dance begins again
in a different
rhythm

Kathleen Hollingworth

Cock Pheasant, Hare and Fox

Has Time Healed?

I'm often asked 'Has time healed?'. Time has put a distance between the event of Ben's death and the present time but it hasn't healed. Part of me died with Ben the evening of the 3rd February 1998 and I realise that from a six year perspective it will never return. My strong roots have grown other shoots and there are other wonderful people in my life but the cut was too savage and deep to heal completely. I can never be as strong as I was before my beloved son's death. I am easily reduced to tears and know my limitations.

I have become better at spotting bad days on the horizon and these are not always the obvious ones such as Christmas, Ben's birthday and the date of his death. Sometimes I am caught off guard and am inconsolable when I see the steady rise of smoke from heather burning, or worse smell it. However, I have also learnt to be kind to myself and not expect too much from either myself or other people and I try never to become overtired as this is a sure way to induce uncontrollable tears.

It Was Beautiful

It was beautiful
As long as it lasted
The journey of my life.

I have no regrets
Whatsoever save
The pain I'll leave behind.

Farewell my friends
I smile and bid you goodbye.
No, shed no tears,
For I need them not.
All I need is your smile.

If you feel sad
Do think of me
For that's what I like.
When you live in the hearts
Of those you love
Remember then -
You never die.

Words of Gitanjali,
an Indian teenager, who wrote this
shortly before her own death from cancer.

74

Ben with 'tame' grouse

Photograph taken on Grinton Moor by Tony Williams - a friend and former colleague of Ben

What has helped?

In the early days nothing at all seemed to help and yet now as I look back I realise how family and friends were helping by standing by and taking their cue from us. They were quietly waiting to hold me if I fell, always there to listen if I needed to talk, there to walk the many miles with me as I searched for Ben. I had a handful of very special people who would listen as I poured out the same thoughts over and over again, dissecting and investigating every aspect of Ben's death, then doing it all over again the following day. They would never tire of listening to me and even today if I need to talk through some new slant on it all they are there. That is true friendship.

I am forever grateful to these dear people who also had their own grief to deal with but always put me and my family first.

It helps to see the remembrance flowers on his grave at the anniversary of his death and his birthday and also the Christmas wreaths, some hand made. There are sometimes kind words written on cards and left with the flowers. I am always moved when I see the lone poppy left on his grave after the remembrance day service at Arkengarthdale Church by a thoughtful friend.

It helps to have a place of work to go every day although in the early days, if I hadn't needed the money, I believe I would have handed in my notice. This would have been entirely the wrong thing to do but at the time I felt I could not and did not want to be in a place that held so many reminders. Working at the village school is now a comfort to me but I was distraught the first time the children sang 'All Things Bright and Beautiful' in an assembly shortly after returning to work as this was sung at Ben's funeral.

I did have a few sessions of counselling but this did not work for me simply because I was able to pour out my innermost feelings to my friends. They were my counsellors. When this is not possible then I do believe counselling has an important role to play.

A dear lady, who now is sadly dead, touched my arm gently the first time I ventured out with my family for a meal at the local pub and said, "You've had a rough ride lass" No other words were needed. This helped.

We had a Christmas card printed from an etching Ben had done at Arkengarthdale School called 'Winter at Sealhouses' It was the last Christmas card we sent which coincided with the millennium. We now give our Christmas card money to charity every year. This helps. Every day I try to do at least one positive thing in remembrance of my beloved son and in this way he lives on.

Very soon after Ben's death I was put in touch with The Compassionate Friends, an organisation founded to help bereaved parents, and this has proved an invaluable source of help. They have a postal library which is run by a lady called Catharine Pointer who turned to life again after her daughter died in an accident and she was left in a wheelchair. She has been an inspiration to me and her kind notes sent with my library books every few weeks have given me enormous strength. You know when reading the quarterly newsletters that here are people who totally understand the pain of losing a child or children from whatever cause and at whatever age.

Yet the one thing that has helped us most as a family is the acknowledgement of the enormity of our loss. I also lost my father to suicide and at the time felt the pain was off the scale but knew the loss of a child would be worse. Just how much worse I couldn't have imagined in my wildest thoughts and yet the love I had for my father could not have been greater. A parent dies and it is the past, a child dies and part of the future dies too.

Grey Partridge

'Winter at Sealhouses' - etching by Ben aged 10

Ben's Dog Brock

Death My friend

Death
my friend
Were you ever the enemy?
I think not
Only the fear
that you would take my child
and this you did
So simple
We all live
We all die
It's only timing

Kathleen Hollingworth

Going On

'To everything there is a season, and a time to every purpose under the Heaven'
Ecclesiastes 3:1

When Ben died my family and I entered a new era and were transported into a strange, dark land where there was no light for many months. We lived in the same house, same dale and had the same people around us but so dreadful was the change in our lives that we barely recognised ourselves in this darkness. I remember Reverend Peter Midwood saying to my husband and I before Ben's funeral that the life we had known had gone forever. It could never come back and as hard as that was we had to accept it as a fact.

This book has reflected the many stages I have gone through and the hope I eventually found to go on and live life to its fullest again. It has purposely been my reflections. In no way do they detract from the pain and suffering my husband and sons have gone through and still go through. Their pain has matched mine every step of the way but their pain is another story.

In the days after Ben's death I would look in the mirror and was surprised at how normal I looked. Why were there no open wounds, gouges and deep cuts? Now I look into the mirror and don't recognise the woman looking back at me. To everyone else I am sure I look much the same but to me this woman is a different person to the woman I knew in early February 1998. I can see the pain and it reassures me that it has been recorded in me.

Memories of those appalling early days are etched into me with deep clarity. I talk as if that time and now are separate. This isn't the case.

What happened on the 3rd February 1998 has been grafted into me and will never be separate just as my son cannot be separated. He was part of me once and will be for all time. We are inextricably connected and I am glad of that.

How am I now from a six year perspective? I am alive but more importantly I want to be alive. Although now I can never see a sunset, one of those breathtaking skies where the pink and gold ripples go on forever and you lose yourself in the intenseness of it for a moment until it begins to fade, without seeing my son sitting in his Landrover immersed in a 'sunset glow' about to die. Why he chose that time to die I probably will never know. Perhaps it was easier to go with the moment than return to life with all its ordinariness and problems.

I have never felt any anger at Ben or a need to forgive what he did. I have always felt the greatest compassion imaginable and this only grows as the years pass. I know anger can be a normal part of the grieving process but am glad I did not have to deal with this emotion on top of all the others.

I have three sons and feel exceptionally blessed at knowing these people. Two are physically with me, one is spiritually with me. To have never known Ben would have been a far greater pain than the pain of his death. I believe we all have a time to live and a time to die. Ben's time was the last quarter of the twentieth century.

I go on because I have no choice but I do go on valuing my family and friends and being loving and compassionate to my fellow human beings and fellow creatures a little more. In fact I carry on much as I did before but I attach no importance to possessions and all importance to family and friendships.

Idyll

In the grey summer garden I shall find you
With day-break and the morning hills behind you.
There will be rain-wet roses; stir of wings;
And down the wood a thrush that wakes and sings.
Not from the past you'll come, but from that deep
Where beauty murmurs to the soul asleep:
And I shall know the sense of life re-born
From dreams into the mystery of morn
Where gloom and brightness meet. And standing there
Till that calm song is done, at last we'll share
The league-spread, quiring symphonies that are
Joy in the world, and peace, and dawn's one star.

Siegfried Sassoon

Mistlethrush

Gifts

"Look!" you said. And I saw the storm clouds heap and roll and darken and the sky turn blue and the silver lightning tear the dark from top to bottom.

"Look!" And I saw the geese go by, beating their wings against the evening air, and calling to one another as they passed.

"Look!" And I saw the stillness of a lake erupt to a shimmering of fishes, chasing the crumbs you'd thrown.

"Look!" And I saw a sky peppered with stars. And the glitter of frost on every blade of grass.

"Look!" And I saw the little things I might have missed. The pods of scarlet pimpernel, the fine-wire legs of a sociable robin, and his understanding eye, the whirls in the ear of a kitten, and the dew-spangled webs of spiders strewn across the hedge, the dip and dart of damselflies, the scampering of beetles, the quiver of a mouses's whiskers, the snub green nose of a hyacinth shoving through the soil.

You gave me food and warmth and love.

And you gave me stars.

Rosanne Ambrose Brown

Ben bought me a book 'In Praise of Mothers' for Christmas 1995.
'Gifts' is a poem from the book.

Geese in flight

Photograph by permission of Anita Torstenson

I will not forget you...
I have held you in the palm of my hand.
Isaiah 49:15

Acknowledgements

Gifts - Rosanne Ambrose-Brown: From A Special Collection in Praise of Mothers, published by Exley Publications Ltd. Used with permission.

Walking Away - C Day Lewis: Published by Sinclair-Stevenson (1992) Copyright © 1992 in this edition The Estate of C Day Lewis. Reprinted by permission of The Random House Group Ltd.

To My Son - Dorothea Eastwood: Reprinted by kind permission of Hugo Eastwood.

To the Memory of Rupert Brooke - W W Gibson: Reprinted by permission of Macmillan UK.

To My Mountain - Kathleen Raine: Reprinted by permission of Golgonooza Press.

I Shall Find You - Siegfried Sassoon: Copyright Siegfried Sassoon by kind permission of George Sassoon.

Time Does Not Bring Relief - Edna St Vincent Millay: From Collected Poems, HarperCollins. Copyright 1917, 1945 by Edna St. Vincent Millay. All rights reserved. Reprinted by permission of Elizabeth Barnett, literary executor.

Fire In My Heart, Ice In My Veins - David Traisman: Copyright 1992. Reprinted with permission from Centering Corporation, Omaha, Nebraska, 402-553-1200.

It Was Beautiful - Gitanjali: Copyright The Society for Promoting Christian Knowledge by kind permission of Mo Dingle.

Every effort has been made to trace the copyright holders of material quoted. Information on any omissions should be sent to the publisher who will make full acknowledgement in any future edition.